Clarity Simplicity Success

A Self Coaching Journal for Women

JACQUI ALDER

Hi, I'm Jacqui Alder and I've developed this self-coaching journal to help women create their own path to success while remaining true to themselves. It's intended to apply equally to your personal and professional lives.

The journal brings together my knowledge and experience gained over the past 30 years as a coach, consultant, and executive.

As women, we often tread a fine line trying to balance competing expectations about what success is. Sometimes, trying to live up to those expectations takes us off course.

What would you do if you had a blank slate and could define what success means for you? This journal is that blank slate.

Yes, we all have practical realities which may constrain us, but we also have the freedom to choose what we do in the space that's left.

My career – like my life – has taken a long, winding road, but now that I've found my path I can see the importance of all the twists, turns, and missteps I've experienced. But I do wish I had some more help along the way. Don't get me wrong: I'm glad I experienced those twists, turns, and missteps because they made me who I am today. However, with the benefit of some guidance, the younger Jacqui may not have suffered so many sprained ankles, blistered heels or stones in her shoes while treading her path.

...create their own path to success while remaining true to themselves.

As a coach, I've learned how to guide others to find their answers by listening to their inner voice. Importantly, I've also learned that taking one step forward is more empowering than setting audacious, and often unrealistic, goals.

I understand that, for whatever reason, not every woman can, or wants to, hire a coach. That's why I created this journal – I want to share my knowledge with, and guide, women who I may not get the honour to coach personally. I want to help you define what success means to you, to create your own path to that success, and to walk it.

The self-coaching process will guide you through each step which you can work through at your own pace.

I hope you find using the journal a practical, encouraging, challenging, and empowering experience which helps you take steps towards creating a future that's right for you.

You can find out more about me at the back of this journal, or on my website **www.claritysimplicitysuccess.com.**

PURPOSE OF THIS JOURNAL

Have you lost sight of why you're doing what you're currently doing?

Are you at a cross-road and uncertain of where you're heading?

For women, getting the **balance** right between **being successful** and being **true to yourself** requires us to tread a fine line. This is partly because conventional definitions of success tend to have a masculine twist. It's hard to feel successful when what you're doing, or how you're doing it, feel inauthentic.

I've felt this way in the past and I wish I knew then what I know now. That's why I designed this journal specifically for women – for you.

This journal will guide you through the discovery, creation, and achievement of your success.

This journal is designed to help women create their own definition of success and to work towards achieving it.

STRUCTURE & DESIGN

Structure

This journal is divided into four main sections:

Clarity Describe who you are and identify what's important to you.

Simplicity Identify your skills, interests, and motivators.

Success Define what success means for you and take steps to achieve it.

Reflection Record important learnings and discoveries you have.

Design

There are exercises throughout the first three sections, some of which involve speaking to friends, family, or colleagues. I encourage you to share your progress with someone you trust, even if the exercise doesn't specify it. Sharing your progress and getting feedback helps clarify **your truth**.

Scattered throughout the sections are outline drawings. These are for colouring in, if you feel like it.

This journal is lineless because it's your space to create what you want. You can write, draw, or paste things onto its pages.

HOW TO USE THIS JOURNAL

Outlined below is my guidance for using this journal, however, you can choose to use it in whichever way works best for you.

The content of this journal is your coach. It will guide you through the discovery, creation, and achievement of your success.

Self-Coaching Process

The first three sections of this journal are based upon the coaching process I use with my clients:

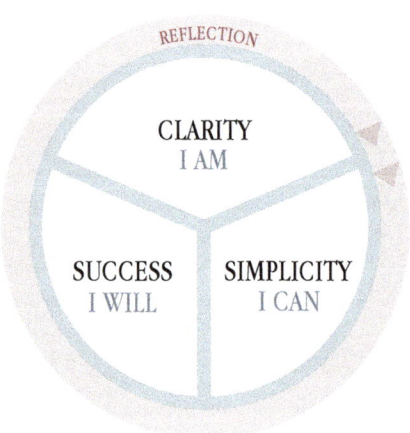

Clarity: Start here

The exercises in this section are designed to help you define who you are and what's important to you. I suggest you start here because this definition is the cornerstone to all that follows. After all, this is all about you. Refer to your definition as you work through the other sections. You might also find that you return to this section and change your definition as you get more clarity. That's okay.

Simplicity: Follows Clarity

The exercises in this section are designed to help you identify your interests, skills, and motivators. You'll use this information to decide where you want to focus your energy.

Success: Follows Simplicity

This section will bring it all together. You'll decide what success means to you, your goals, and what you're going to do to achieve them. Importantly, this is where you start working towards your success.

Reflection: Use It Anytime

As you work through these sections you'll have achievements, hit barriers, have 'aha! moments' and learn things about yourself. This section is for recording these events, as well as for writing down any reflections you may have as you go along. Dive into it whenever you need to.

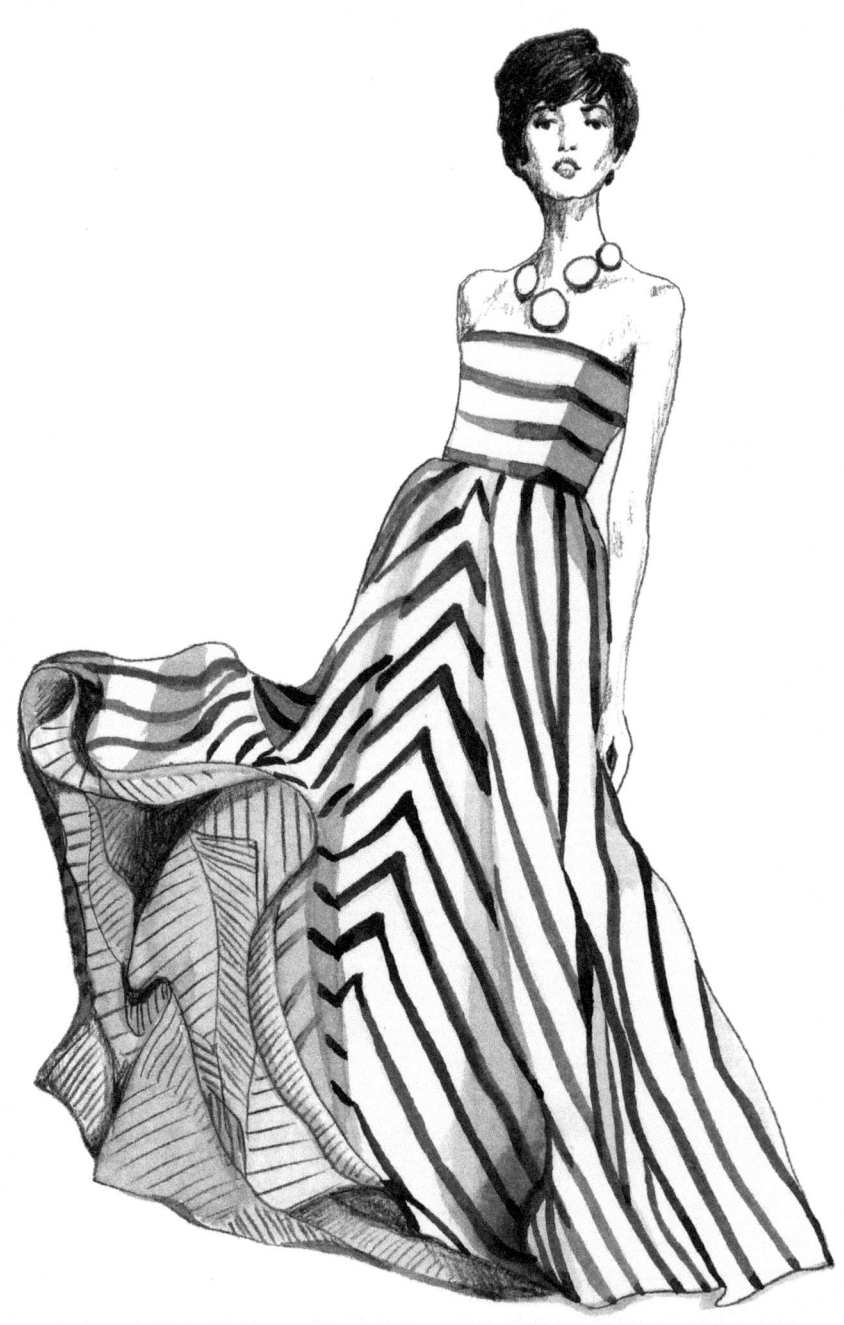

Let's start creating your success!

SOME WORDS OF REASSURANCE

You've taken on a personally challenging task which has the potential to create positive change by putting you in the driver's seat of your life. You may feel excitement, doubt, fear, and a variety of mixed emotions as you work through. Conversely, you may find the process quite straight forward.

Whatever you experience or decide as a result of working through this journal is okay. Suspend any self-judgement because nothing is either right or wrong, or good or bad; it just is. The purpose is to help you tune into yourself, make decisions, and take actions that are right for you at this point in time.

You don't have to do this on your own. Reach out to others for feedback and support.

If you're still stuck, you can also head over to the section titled What Do I Do If I'm Not Making Progress? You'll find it listed in the index. Don't forget to visit the www.claritysimplicitysuccess.com website for articles and resources.

'Choose your steps wisely because your footprints may be followed by others.' JACQUI ALDER

CONTENTS

CLARITY	12
SIMPLICITY	40
SUCCESS	74
What Do I Do If I'm Not Making Progress	130
REFLECTION	134
My Hopes For You	157

'In order to be yourself, you must first know who you are.'

JACQUI ALDER

Clarity

CLARITY

The exercises in this section are designed to help you define who you are and what's important to you at this point in your life. Your task is to work through the clarifying questions / exercises to help you find your definition.

I encourage you to use drawings, colour, and paste clippings to bring your answers to life.

NOTE

As you work through this journal, pay careful attention to your inner voice and thoughts. Stay alert for your inner critic; it may try to throw you off track by inserting things you don't truly intend.

One clue that your inner critic is at play is its use of the word 'should'. If you catch it doing this, stop, and pay attention because if you try to ignore it, it'll just keep nagging you.

When my inner critic pipes up I write down what it says. I then acknowledge the message and tell myself **what I will do**. For example, if my inner critic says, 'you should get up' but I decide I need more rest, I tell myself 'I choose to get more sleep'.

If you still have trouble silencing your inner critic, try using the **Reflection** section.

If none of these things work, reach out to someone for support.

❶ What's important
TO YOU?

Go with what's in your heart. There's no judgement here, just your truth.

As you answer this question, make sure you also consider your current life circumstances. We all deal with the practical realities of life, and there are always things you just have to do.

❷ What's not important TO YOU?

These are things that you know you don't want to put energy into – unless you really have to. It's important to identify them because doing so will help you to better understand yourself.

Keep writing until you've exhausted the list.

Review what you've written. What are the themes?
Write them down.

CLARITY

❸ Identify your
CORE VALUES.

Read the list below and mark the 10 values that are most important to you.

ACHIEVEMENT	ADVENTURE	AUTHENTICITY
AUTHORITY	AUTONOMY	BALANCE
BEAUTY / AESTHETICS	CHALLENGE	COMMUNITY
COMPASSION	COMPETENCE	COURAGE
CREATIVITY	CURIOSITY	ENJOYMENT / FUN
FAIRNESS	FAME	FAMILY
FRIENDSHIP	GROWTH	HAPPINESS
HEALTH / FITNESS	HELP OTHERS / SERVICE	HONESTY
HUMOUR	INFLUENCE	INNER HARMONY
INTEGRITY	JUSTICE	KINDNESS
KNOWLEDGE	LOVE	LOYALTY
OPENNESS	OPTIMISM	ORDER
PEACE	POPULARITY	RECOGNITION
REPUTATION	RESPECT	RESPONSIBILITY
SECURITY	SELF-RESPECT	SPIRITUALITY
STABILITY	STATUS	TRUST
VARIETY	WEALTH	WISDOM

NOTE: Women who reflect on their core values perform better. It enhances their sense of self-worth and reduces the negative impact of stereotypes. When you do this exercise, make sure you are listening to yourself to ensure the values you choose are your own.

Review the top 10 values you marked on the previous page. Identify the 5 which are most important to you. List each value here, followed by the words '… is important to me because …' and then add whatever your 'because' statement is.

❹ What did you learn
ABOUT YOURSELF?

Look back over your answers to questions 1, 2 and 3. Reflect upon the process and note anything important that you learned about yourself.

'What does being true to yourself mean for you?'

JACQUI ALDER

❺ What does being
TRUE TO YOURSELF MEAN FOR YOU?

In this exercise, you will create your Clarity description by defining what being true to yourself means for you. This will provide the foundation for the rest of the self-coaching process.

Use the space below before completing the exercise on the following pages. Write, draw, or paste anything which you feel is important. Here are some questions to prompt you.

What emotions have you experienced?

What themes have you noticed so far?

Did anything grab your attention?

When you're ready, turn the page, and create your Clarity description.

MY CLARITY DESCRIPTION

Being true to myself means …'

When I am being this way I feel …'

When you're 80% satisfied with your
Clarity description, STOP.

❻ When you're 80% satisfied,
PAUSE, REFLECT, AND SHARE IT. But not for too long.

If you need to, go back to your Clarity description, and make any adjustments.

Use the Reflection section to record any important realisations or learnings you may want to refer to later. Remember to use this section as you work through this journal. I'm hoping it will become a treasure trove of personal insight for you.

When you're feeling 80% ready to keep going, turn the page to see what's next. I suggest this because it's easy to get stuck if you stop moving. Momentum is important.

I'll keep reminding you of this as you go through the journal.

BEFORE WE MOVE ON ...

Congratulate yourself because you've done a lot of work to this point.

Your Clarity description is your compass, and it'll help you navigate through the voyage ahead. Refer to it regularly, particularly if you feel you've lost your way. You may find you need to adjust it, and that's okay – it's your truth.

The next section is Simplicity. In it you'll identify your interests, skills, and motivators. This information, along with your Clarity description, will help you decide where you want to focus your energy.

'Simply be yourself and be yourself simply.'

JACQUI ALDER

Simplicity

SIMPLICITY

The exercises in this section are designed to help you identify your skills, interests, and motivators. You'll use this information to decide where you want to focus your energy.

Your task is to work through the clarifying questions / exercises to help you identify your skills, interests, and motivators.

Before you start working on this section, review your Clarity description because this'll help you stay on course. Refer to it as often as you need to. Remember to listen to yourself carefully as you work through because your inner critic may try to sneak in (remember, listen for it using the word 'should').

NOTE **Career interests and gender.**
There's evidence of differences in career interests between men and women. However, these differences explain just 30% of the variance in male / female representation in careers. Gender stereotypes are thought to play a significant role in the discrepancy. Women internalise gender stereotypes, apply them to themselves and to other women. The result being, women unwittingly hold themselves back.

As you go through these exercises, ask yourself: 'Am I applying a stereotype / gender expectation to myself?'

SKILLS

① What are you GOOD AT?

What do you 'know' you're good at?

What have you practiced or worked hard on to improve your skill level?

❷ What do you believe you COULD BE GOOD AT?

What do you feel you have a natural talent for?

What are you currently skilled at that you could develop or apply differently?

'Simplicity is liberating your heart from the confines of your mind.' JACQUI ALDER

❸ What do others THINK?

Select some people who know you from different contexts (e.g. family, social, and professional).

a. Ask them what they think you *are* good at. Get them to give examples. Clarify by asking them why they think so.

b. Then ask what they think you *could* be good at.

❹ Compare your results with the
RESULTS FROM OTHERS.

Are good at:

ME

OTHERS

Could be good at:

ME

OTHERS

Note the following:

SIMILARITIES

DIFFERENCES

SURPRISES

THEMES

INTERESTS

❺ What are you CURIOUS ABOUT?

❻ What energises YOU?

❼ What are you
MOTIVATED TO DO?

If you are, or could be, good at something AND it sparks your curiosity and / or energises you, you're more likely to be motivated to do it.

If you're motivated to do something, you're more likely to be successful at it. You'll have more energy for it, and you'll be more likely to persist when you encounter obstacles.

Review your Skills identification summary from Exercise 4, along with your answers to Interests Exercises 5 and 6. Then turn to the following page. Here you will summarise what you're curious about and energised by.

'*Motivation is the triumph of hope over fear, interest over apathy, and spirit over will.*'

JACQUI ALDER

Could be good at:

CURIOUS ABOUT

ENERGISED BY

Are good at:

CURIOUS ABOUT

ENERGISED BY

SIMPLICITY

⑧ Where do you want to
FOCUS YOUR ENERGY?

In this exercise, you're going to Simplify where you'll focus your energy as you continue to work through this self-coaching process. This is important preparation for your work in the Success section.

You'll do this by choosing 3 of the skills / interests you've identified in the previous exercise. The purpose being to tap into your positive energy by working on things which you're either energised by, or curious about, or both.

Are you ready? Okay, now go back and review the results of the previous exercise.

Choose the top 3 skills / interests you want to pursue further. It's perfectly acceptable to pick things you might need to learn or practice. There's no right or wrong, this is your choice.

When you're ready, write your choices in the space provided here and on the following pages. Include the reasons behind your choice by adding a 'because' statement. Here's one of my current focus areas as an example:

> Learn how to sketch because I want to increase my creativity.

NOTE This journal will refer to your work in this exercise as your 'Simplicity description' in future sections.

MY SIMPLICITY DESCRIPTION

MY SIMPLICITY DESCRIPTION

MY SIMPLICITY DESCRIPTION

When you're 80% satisfied with your Simplicity description, STOP.

9 When you're done, pause,

CHECK YOUR SIMPLICITY DESCRIPTION FOR CONSISTENCY WITH YOUR CLARITY DESCRIPTION.

If you need to, go back to your Clarity or Simplicity descriptions, and make any adjustments.

Take some time to reflect, but not too long because momentum is important.

When you're feeling 80% ready to keep going, turn the page to see what's next.

BEFORE WE MOVE ON ...

Congratulations! You persisted and now you've completed two of the three parts of the process.

Firstly, you described what being true to yourself means in your Clarity description.

In the current section, you've identified your skills, interests, and motivators. Using your Clarity description as a guide, you've chosen three skills / interests you wish to focus on. Finally, you've created your Simplicity description by expanding upon the reasons you chose those three things.

The next section is Success. In it you'll bring everything together. Using your Clarity and Simplicity descriptions as guides, you'll define what Success looks like for you, take stock of where you are now, identify the next steps you need to take, and start working towards your Success.

The work in the Success section requires you to make commitments to yourself, and to take action. Before we move on, I have serious questions for you.

Are you committed to seeing this through?

Are you prepared to do whatever it takes?

Are you sure?

Okay, let's go!

'*Success is yours to define, not for others to prescribe.*'

JACQUI ALDER

Success

SUCCESS

In this section you'll bring everything together by defining what Success means to you at this point in time; by taking stock of where you are now, and by identifying the next steps to take. Refer to your Clarity and Simplicity descriptions regularly as you go along because they are your guides.

Working through these exercises may provoke some strong feelings. To help you stay centred, use the Reflection section. Reach out to someone for support if you need to.

The future is a product of what we do and don't do. It's time to create your future.

❶ Create your
SUCCESS STATEMENT / PICTURE.

Review your Clarity and Simplicity descriptions.

I recommend that you build your statement / picture in four stages. Describe, draw, or create a collage of:

- How you'll BE when you are successful.
- What you'll DO when you are successful.
- What you'll HAVE as a result.
- How you'll FEEL.

Make your statement / picture clear and powerful because this is what you're working towards – your destination for this trip. Be patient because it may take a bit of re-work before you're happy with it. If you choose to write it, I recommend using colours and symbols to highlight key elements so it'll be more memorable.

SUCCESS

❷ Take a break.
REFLECT. SHARE.

Congratulations! You have done a lot of work to get this far.

Now, reward yourself with a short break to let it all sink in. Use the Reflection section to record any important realisations or learnings. Discuss your Success with others because doing so will help to reinforce and clarify its meaning for you.

❸ Have you already achieved the
SUCCESS YOU WANT?

IF YOUR ANSWER IS **YES** THEN CONGRATULATIONS.

I figure this a new realisation for you. If so, take time to reflect on what you've learned and what this realisation means for you.

IF YOUR ANSWER IS **NO**, THEN CONGRATULATIONS FOR ALL THE WORK YOU'VE DONE TO GET THIS FAR.

You've created the design specifications for your immediate future, so you can now go on to build a success that's right for you at this point in your life.

When you're ready, we'll start the building process.

❹ Take stock.
WHERE ARE YOU NOW?

Review your Success description and compare it to the present. Describe how things are for you right now in relation to each element.

How am I BEING?

What am I DOING?

What do I HAVE as a result?

How do I FEEL?

After you've completed this, you'll know your starting point. You're heading off from here towards destination Success.

❺ What's been
HOLDING YOU BACK?

Complete the following statement in the journal, and repeat it as many times as you need to until you run out of answers.

I haven't achieved my Success because … '

> **NOTE**
>
> **A word on gender differences and career aspirations.**
>
> Women are as ambitious as men. Roughly equal numbers of men and women say they want to be promoted. However, alignment of values is more important to women than men. Women are more likely than men to put their values ahead of their career.

'The key to achieving anything is to start, take one step at a time and to keep going.' JACQUI ALDER

❻ What action will you take to achieve YOUR SUCCESS?

You might be feeling a bit daunted by now. Relax. We'll get there one step at a time.

In this exercise, we're going to walk through the process to plan your first steps to Success. Yes, we're going to go through it step by step!

By doing this you'll get familiar with the procedure. This is important because once you've completed your first steps, you'll repeat this process until you're satisfied you've reached your destination.

Let's start planning your first footsteps.

Review your work in this section so far, then choose three priority areas to focus on. Write these below:

Once you're done, ask yourself the following question for each priority area, and enter your answers in the space provided:

What's the right next step for me to take?

Keep it realistic because you're going to take one small step at a time. Once you've completed a step, you'll assess the view from there, and then you'll decide where to step next.

Well done! You've decided your priorities and the next steps to take. Here are some questions to assist you to identify what help you may need to take those steps. Enter your answers into the space provided.

What help do I need? Who can help me?

Okay, we're almost there. The last step in the process is to decide when you'll have finished taking your first steps. This is intended to motivate you, and to make you accountable – to yourself.

My promise to myself: When will I do this by?

When you're finished you'll have your 3 x 3:

- 3 priority areas to focus on;
- 3 actions to take as a next step (including what / whose help you need);
- 3 promises to yourself about when you'll complete your actions.

Once you're done, review your 3 x 3, and make any changes. Then come back here because we've got some things to do before you move into action.

WELCOME BACK.

Well done! You've laid out the first stepping stones on the path to your Success.

I've created some pages to help you track your progress, and to keep going. After this exercise you'll find 3 sets of pages titled My Progress - one for each priority area. Use them to record your 3 x 3, track your progress, and plan your next steps.

Tracking your progress is important because it helps you keep focused, feel a sense of achievement, and identify when you're stuck.

Momentum is vital - you may have noticed I've mentioned this a few times already. To sustain your momentum, I recommend you …

Check in on your progress every day.

At the end of every day, take a few minutes to read over your 3 x 3, and to ask yourself this question for each priority area:

Did I do my best to make progress toward achieving this?

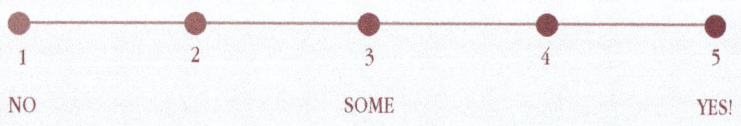

1 — NO
2
3 — SOME
4
5 — YES!

If it helps, write notes in the space provided in the progress pages.

I recommend you enlist the help of someone you trust. Having to answer to someone else is a great motivator.

If you haven't done your best, forgive yourself. Then, figure out what stopped you, and ask yourself what's the right next step?

When you've completed an action, keep on taking steps until you get where you're going.

Once you've completed an action, give yourself a pat on the back, and then ask yourself the questions you used to build your 3 x 3. That is:

What's the right next step for me to take?

What help do I need? Who can help me?

My promise to myself: When will I do this by?

Repeat this process until you're satisfied that you've reached your goal.

Are you ready to start work?

Great! Start by transferring your 3 x 3 to the My Progress pages. Remember, there's one set for each priority area. To make sure you've got plenty of room, each set has a few pages.

NOTES

My
PROGRESS

What's the right next step for me to take?

What help do I need? Who can help me?

PRIORITY AREA  _____

My promise to myself: When will I do this by?

Did I do my best to make progress toward achieving this?

○ 5 YES!

4

○ 3 SOME

2

○ 1 NO

NOTES

My
PROGRESS

What's the right next step for me to take?

What help do I need? Who can help me?

PRIORITY AREA 1 ▷ _____

My promise to myself: When will I do this by?

Did I do my best to make progress toward achieving this?

○ 5 YES!
4
○ 3 SOME
2
○ 1 NO

NOTES

My
PROGRESS

What's the right next step for me to take?

What help do I need? Who can help me?

PRIORITY AREA 1  _____

My promise to myself: When will I do this by?

Did I do my best to make progress toward achieving this?

○ 5 YES!

4

○ 3 SOME

2

○ 1 NO

NOTES

My
PROGRESS

What's the right next step for me to take?

What help do I need? Who can help me?

PRIORITY AREA 1 ▷ _____

My promise to myself: When will I do this by?

Did I do my best to make progress toward achieving this?

○ 5   YES!
  4
○ 3   SOME
  2
○ 1   NO

NOTES

My
PROGRESS

What's the right next step for me to take?

What help do I need? Who can help me?

PRIORITY AREA 1 _____

My promise to myself: When will I do this by?

Did I do my best to make progress toward achieving this?

○ 5 YES!
 4
○ 3 SOME
 2
○ 1 NO

NOTES
My
PROGRESS

What's the right next step for me to take?

What help do I need? Who can help me?

PRIORITY AREA 2 ▷ _____

My promise to myself: When will I do this by?

Did I do my best to make progress toward achieving this?

○ 5 YES!

4

○ 3 SOME

2

○ 1 NO

NOTES

My
PROGRESS

What's the right next step for me to take?

What help do I need? Who can help me?

PRIORITY AREA 2 _____

My promise to myself: When will I do this by?

Did I do my best to make progress toward achieving this?

○ 5 YES!

4

○ 3 SOME

2

○ 1 NO

My NOTES
PROGRESS

What's the right next step for me to take?

What help do I need? Who can help me?

PRIORITY AREA 2 ▷ _____

My promise to myself: When will I do this by?

Did I do my best to make progress toward achieving this?

○ 5 YES!

4

○ 3 SOME

2

○ 1 NO

NOTES
My
PROGRESS

What's the right next step for me to take?

What help do I need? Who can help me?

PRIORITY AREA 2  _____

My promise to myself: When will I do this by?

Did I do my best to make progress toward achieving this?

○ 5 YES!
  4
○ 3 SOME
  2
○ 1 NO

NOTES
My
PROGRESS

What's the right next step for me to take?

What help do I need? Who can help me?

PRIORITY AREA 2 ▷ _____

My promise to myself: When will I do this by?

Did I do my best to make progress toward achieving this?

○ 5 YES!
  4
○ 3 SOME
  2
○ 1 NO

NOTES

My
PROGRESS

What's the right next step for me to take?

What help do I need? Who can help me?

PRIORITY AREA 3 > _____

My promise to myself: When will I do this by?

Did I do my best to make progress toward achieving this?

○ 5 YES!
  4
○ 3 SOME
  2
○ 1 NO

NOTES

My
PROGRESS

What's the right next step for me to take?

What help do I need? Who can help me?

PRIORITY AREA 3 _____

My promise to myself: When will I do this by?

Did I do my best to make progress toward achieving this?

○ 5 YES!
4
○ 3 SOME
2
○ 1 NO

NOTES

My
PROGRESS

What's the right next step for me to take?

What help do I need? Who can help me?

PRIORITY AREA 3 ▷ _____

My promise to myself: When will I do this by?

Did I do my best to make progress toward achieving this?

○ 5 YES!

4

○ 3 SOME

2

○ 1 NO

NOTES
My
PROGRESS

What's the right next step for me to take?

What help do I need? Who can help me?

PRIORITY AREA 3 ▷ _____

My promise to myself: When will I do this by?

Did I do my best to make progress toward achieving this?

○ 5 YES!

4

○ 3 SOME

2

○ 1 NO

NOTES

My
PROGRESS

What's the right next step for me to take?

What help do I need? Who can help me?

PRIORITY AREA 3> _____

My promise to myself: When will I do this by?

Did I do my best to make progress toward achieving this?

○ 5   YES!

   4

○ 3   SOME

   2

○ 1   NO

What do I do if I'm not
MAKING PROGRESS?

If you run out of motivation, check in with yourself by asking these questions:

Is this what I really want?

Am I willing to do what it takes to get there?

If you answer no, then stop and decide where you go to from here. It's okay if you decide to stop. It's your life. That's the point of this journal: you're doing **what's right for you right now**.

If you answer **yes**, then you may need some extra support. If you haven't enlisted the help of someone you trust to ask you your daily questions, then now's the time to do it.

Don't forget to visit the www.claritysimplicitysuccess.com website for articles and resources.

A place to record important learnings and discoveries.

Reflection

REFLECTION

MY HOPES FOR YOU

I created this journal for you. It's my way of sharing some of the lessons I've learned from my life experiences, and it's my way to help others succeed on their own terms. As you've been working through the journal, I've been wondering how you're going and hoping the following things for you:

▶ You've found the journal practical, encouraging, challenging and empowering;

▶ You've become more aware of, and comfortable with, what being true to yourself means *for you*, including being perfectly clear about what is important to you right now;

▶ You've identified the things you want to do because they energise you, and by doing so you perhaps added more of them to your life;

▶ You've taken a big step towards creating a future that's right for you;

▶ You've developed a support network of people who know who you are and what you're trying to achieve, and

▶ You feel in control of your future.

Now that you have **Clarity** and **Simplicity** in your mind about what **Success** means for you, take the *new you* out there and fulfil her potential.

You can't give me any greater reward than doing just that.

Clarity
Simplicity
Success™

Copyright ©2017, 2019 Jacqueline Alder

This publication is copyright. Apart from any use as permitted under the Copyright Act 1968, no part may be reproduced without prior written permission from the publisher. Requests and enquiries concerning production and rights should be addressed to Jacqui Alder, hello@claritysimplicitysuccess.com.

Published by Alder Consulting Pty Ltd

Clarity Simplicity Success is a registered Trademark under the Trade Marks Act 1995

ISBN-13:978-0-6486742-0-5

Design by Qalam Design

Illustrations by Emma Francesca

Jacqui Alder is an internationally experienced executive, consultant, and coach who gets a buzz from helping women to flourish.

Jacqui enjoys being of service to women in the community.

She has done this as a member, and board member of several organisations working to advance the status of women.

As director of her own human resources consultancy for 20 years, Jacqui delivered complex change projects for global businesses across a range of industry sectors in various countries.

During her career, Jacqui had personal experience of the inner conflict women feel as they try to balance the expectations of their various roles in life and work.

Now, she applies her skills and experience to empowering other women to be successful at being themselves. It's why she wrote this journal.

Jacqui's qualifications include a Master's Degree in Commerce, which is complemented by several professional accreditations.

I believe we can all succeed – in our own way.

JACQUI ALDER

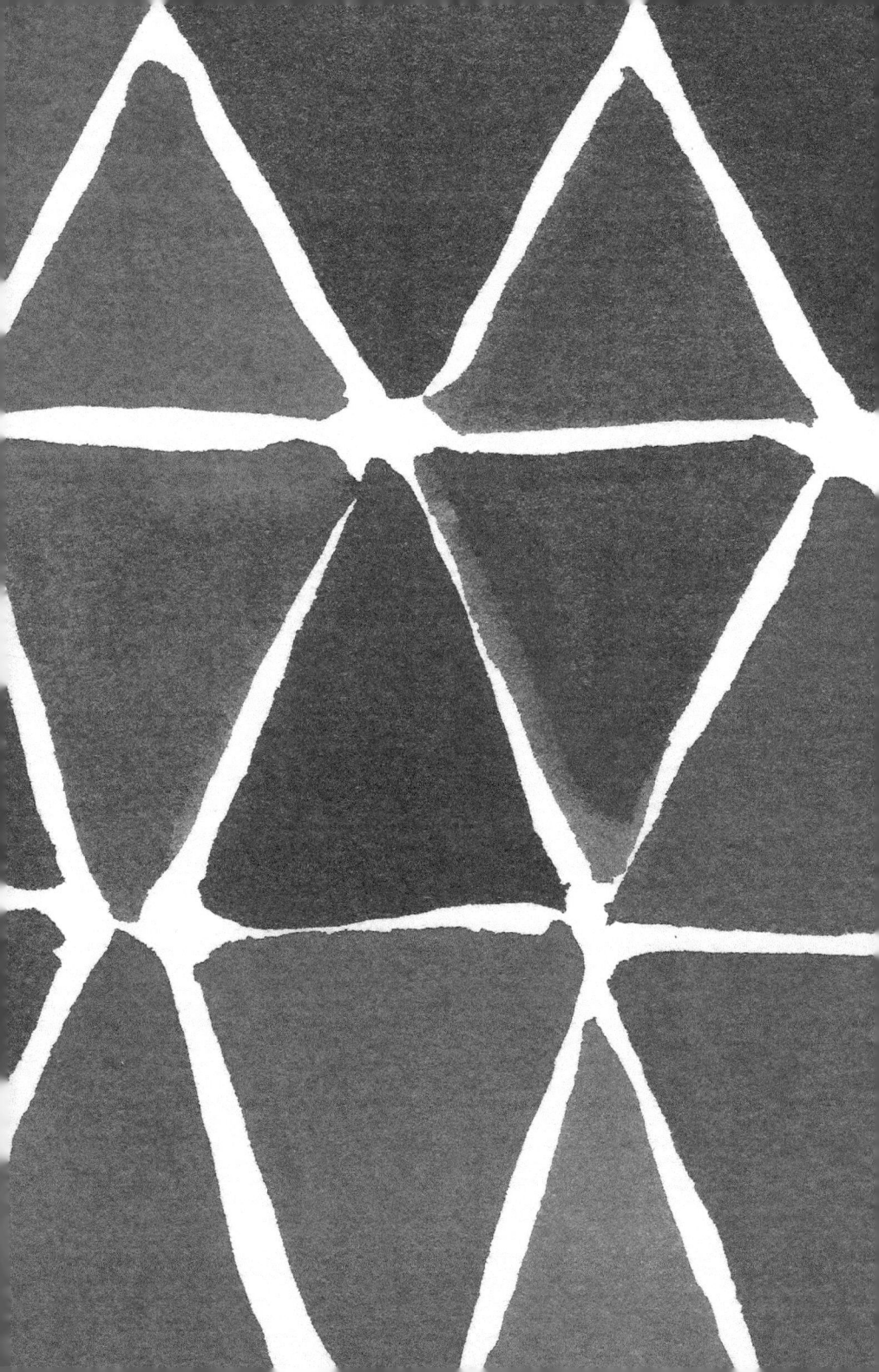

Lightning Source UK Ltd.
Milton Keynes UK
UKHW020120190722
406020UK00001B/38